Gifts

FROM THE

Heart

By Cynthia Whitney Ward

Illustrations By Beth Hendrickson Logan

WINGS BOOKS

New York • Avenel, New Jersey

This 1994 edition is published by Wings Books, distributed by Random House Value Publishing Inc., 40 Engelhard Avenue, Avenel, New Jersey 07001, by arrangement with the author.

Random House
New York · Toronto · London · Sydney · Auckland

Printed and bound in Mexico

Library of Congress Cataloging-in-Publication Data
Ward, Cynthia Whitney.
    Gifts from the heart / by Cynthia Whitney Ward : illustrations
by Beth Hendrickson Logan.
        p.   cm.
    ISBN 0-517-11878-5
      1. Gifts.   I. Title.
GT3050.W37   1995
394—dc20   94-31594
                                                  CIP

8 7 6 5 4 3 2 1

To Caitlin and Jonathan,
my true gifts from the heart

"It is only with the heart that one can see rightly;
what is essential is invisible to the eye."
—Antoine de Saint-Exupery

Contents

Introduction

When I had just moved into a new house, I was delighted to receive a beautifully wrapped gift from my next-door neighbor. My delight turned to enchantment when I discovered a bright blue vase inside with a note attached. It read, "You are invited into my garden each week to pick a bouquet of flowers. Welcome to the neighborhood."

It was the most thoughtful gift anyone had ever given me and, years later, I still treasure the memory of my forays into that lovely garden and the deep friendship that grew from that remarkable gift. Over time, I have come to admire those who can imbue a gift with a bit of themselves, so that the giving, rather than the gift, becomes the true treasure.

The following collection of charming gift ideas has been gathered from friends and acquaintances who indeed have that special talent. I thank them for their generous and thoughtful spirits.

Friendly Gifts

Be a generous gardener! Plant a side garden that will be filled with daisies each summer. When they are all abloom, put up a sign that reads:

Please pick my daisies!

For a friend who enjoys gardening but now finds it a bit too tiring, offer your services for a weekend. Working together can lighten the load, yet give your friend the sense of still being able to work and enjoy his garden. To *wrap* this gift, buy two pairs of inexpensive gardening gloves, tie the wrists together with a bright ribbon and bow, and attach a card on which you've written your gift suggestion.

How about a doubly thoughtful gift for a friend who loves old silver and is an avid gardener? Hunt up an unusual silver pitcher for their home-grown bouquets. For a unique wrapping, use a tarnish-free cloth silver bag. Tie it with a beautiful bow, and add a single fresh flower.

For out-of-town guests, buy postcards of everything that you plan to show them. Also, buy stamps and brightly colored pens. Tie these small tokens with a ribbon and have them waiting in your guests' room.

If you've shared a trip with someone, turn twelve of your favorite snapshots into a wonderful remembrance by placing them in a blank calendar. Make it an even more intimate memento by adding handwritten thoughts about the trip below each photo. For a gift card, use one of the postcards you saved from the trip signed:

Had a wonderful time, glad you were there!

When sending a letter or card to a special friend, tuck a sprig of dried lavender into the envelope before closing and mailing it.

For a friend's extended stay in the hospital, prepare a bowl of beautifully scented potpourri for beside the bed, a pretty travel bag filled with sample-size bottles of lotions and creams, and a small antique hand mirror. Make the wrapping a gift too — tuck everything inside a satin pillowcase.

Ask someone special to tell you all of their favorite things to eat. Then one evening serve them up, crazy combinations and all. Better yet, serve them for breakfast—they'll *never* forget that gift!

If someone has admired your cooking and asked for a recipe, why not surprise her by also including the specific tart pan, cookie cutter, or ingredient that will help her make your recipe perfectly. Wrap this culinary gift in a brightly striped kitchen towel.

If a friend is moving out of town, send a beautiful card to their new address so that it is waiting when they arrive.

If you are moving away and leaving some wonderful friends, buy a stash of flower bulbs. Give a dozen to each friend and keep a dozen for your new home. Come spring, everyone will have a delightful remembrance.

When a favorite author comes to town, take two books to be autographed—one for you, and one for a lucky friend. Wrap this literary gift in the book review that appears in your local paper.

Give a photo party. Everyone should bring an empty photo album or two along with their ever-present box of loose snapshots. Then spend the afternoon or evening getting organized. This is especially great for a rainy or snowy day!

As a thoughtful reminder for someone who has borrowed a special book, tuck a note between the last pages—where he is sure to find it—saying that you hope he enjoyed the book because it was one of your favorites.

When going through a toll booth, pay for the car behind you!

Why do we only send postcards when we are *away*? Buy a handful of lovely cards and send them from home. Tell your faraway friends, "Wish you were *here*."

When buying a gift, think of an endearing habit or trait that is part of your friend's personality, and let that be your guide to buying just the right gift. Do you know someone who always cries at weddings? Give her a beautiful handkerchief. Someone else is a Judy Garland fan? Give her a pair of red shoes.

Gestures can be thoughtful. If you're hosting a dinner party and a guest spills his drink, spill yours. No words will be necessary.

Pampering

AND

Romancing
Gifts

For a charmingly romantic gift, give a small brass compass with a note attached, "Now you will always be able to find your way home." For wrapping paper use a map of your city, with a big red heart drawn around your street. Make sure that your street is visible on the top of the present.

For a sweet twist on giving, why not fashion a *faux* credit card out of handmade paper? You can call it a *DREAM CARD*. Attach a note describing the uniqueness of the card and what it can buy—a weekend for two at a romantic B&B, dinner at the newest restaurant in town, whatever would create the ideal setting for a perfect time away from home.

Pamper a loved one by giving her a basket filled with everything she needs for a relaxing evening at home—a good book, a scented candle, a soothing tape, a bottle of wine, and a few tasty nibbles to help her munch her way through the evening.

Fill a glass jar with thirty slips of paper on which you've written sweet instructions:

Watch the sunset this evening.
Smile, you're beautiful.
Buy a double-dip ice cream cone.

Present this gift to someone special, instructing him to "pull one out each day."

Is there anything more thoughtful or glamorous than sending a dozen roses to someone special? Yes! Sending a dozen roses—each one a different color. Or, just add one flower that is a different color. It could be your signature gift. To complete this theme, wrap the bouquet in several layers of tissue—each a different color. Tie it with a simple white bow.

A fun and inexpensive gift is a packet of lovely gift coupons redeemable for: a hug, running the errands of your choice, a story read aloud, breakfast in bed, etc. The coupons can be written inside blank gift cards that have appropriate illustrations or photos on the front.

Give a gift of time to someone who never seems to have enough of it. Present this busy friend with a calendar on which you've blocked out an afternoon or evening each month. Tell her that she is to go play and you will do her errands, babysit her kids, or do whatever tasks she needs done so that she won't have to.

If you bake a terrific cookie and know someone who delights in them, give this special person a decorative cookie jar or tin for her office, along with a promise to keep it filled each week for a month. Wouldn't this make a perfect birthday gift?

Timing can be everything. Have a cup of steaming hot coffee waiting as your loved one steps from the shower in the morning —especially when he's got a big day ahead.

Serve leftovers on your fine china, and everyone will feel special.

Change the contents of a relaxing basket slightly—with scented bath salts, a relaxation tape, a facial mask, and cocoa, you have a pampering gift for an evening in the bath.

If you will be separated from a loved one for more than a few weeks give him a bar of your favorite soap, so he can begin each day feeling close to you.

A pampering surprise for lucky houseguests: Warm bath towels in the dryer and have them waiting—all toasty and soft —when they step from the bath.

A bubble bath—complete with a glass of champagne waiting on the edge of the tub —can raise anyone's spirits after a particularly miserable day.

When someone needs a little TLC, hide endearing notes in places where she would not expect to find them, but easily will, such as inside a book she's reading, on her car seat, or in her coat pocket. Write these missives on strips of pretty paper, then fold them origami-style (the Japanese paper-folding technique) to make them even more intriguing.

Gifts

OF

Family

Love

For a child's birthday, send a framed picture of his mother or father at the same age.

Surprise a child—or an adult, for that matter—with a birthday breakfast in bed. Fashion a stack of pancakes into a cake, complete with whipped cream and chocolate sauce. Top it all off with lit candles.

For grandparents' birthdays, wrap a present with paper that has been color photocopied to show snapshots of their grandchildren's faces. The kids can make it even more special by writing big X's and O's on the ribbons.

To send a sentimental birthday gift to your grown children, tape yourself singing the lullaby you sang them when they were tiny and pass it along to them.

Write your father or mother—or both—a love letter on Valentine's Day. To create a special envelope, fold a beautiful paper doily around the letter and tie it with a red satin ribbon.

Write Mom a *love* letter on Mother's Day.

Write Dad a *love* letter on Father's Day.

On Mother's Day, think about giving a token gift to *all* the mothers who have touched your life. Find a heart-shaped box, slip in the gift and surround it with candy kisses. This will surely touch their hearts—and yours.

Give a child (or an adult) a Fairy Wand
with a wish list attached. On the list write
dandy things that he or she can have
simply by waving the wand. Include some
treats that you can share, like:

Let's make chocolate chip cookies together.
Want to go to the zoo?
It's your turn to pick the video.

Wrap this magical gift in a gossamer piece
of fabric where you've already tucked some
paper confetti or glitter, to look like fairy
dust.

Gather all of the recipes that your children loved while they were growing up, and hand copy them into a very personal cookbook from mom or dad. Or, photocopy the originals, spills and all.

Send your parents a gift on *your* birthday!

If you have more than one child, take each one on a very special outing all by themselves, without their sibling(s). Plan this time for just the two of you, and continue it each year—even when the children are all grown up and have children of their own.

Surprise your child one day at breakfast. Put food coloring in their milk, and chocolate chips in their cereal. What a fun way to send them off to school on a rainy Monday!

For a little girl, begin a charm bracelet tradition. Create a theme that is special to her or will remind her of you, and send a charm each birthday. Tuck each treasure inside the two halves of a sea shell and tie it with a French ribbon.

Gifts for teens are difficult. Why not pick out an organic body scrub, shampoo, or lotion with a great label and scent and present it each birthday or holiday? Roll the gift inside a glossy fashion magazine and tie it with a big floppy ribbon—with a gift certificate to the magazine attached.

If you sew your children's clothes, save a swatch of fabric from everything that you make them. (You can also do this with your favorite store-bought outfits.) When the time comes, make a beautiful wedding quilt from these saved treasures.

Begin a tradition. When your children are grown and celebrating their first Christmas away from home, wrap something that you saved from their childhood and send it to them. Each Christmas they can look forward to reliving an additional treasured childhood memory. To add a fun twist to these gifts, tuck a token clue to what's inside the box somewhere on the outside—a riddle or poem would do nicely.

For a child's first museum trip, keep them busy with a postcard treasure hunt. In the museum shop buy five postcards that show pictures of museum objects. Have the child find every object during their visit.

"I Do"
Gifts

For the Victorians, a "surprise ball" was a favorite way to wrap a gift. Today, this can be a charming way to pop the question. The idea is to hide the gift—the engagement ring —in the center of a ball that is wound with brightly colored crepe paper strips. Do this by putting the ring in a tiny box, then begin wrapping the paper strips around it (as you would a ball of string). Change colors with each new layer of crepe paper strips. Tuck endearing love notes or token gifts between the layers as you wrap, until you've created a 5- to 6-inch ball. Tie it with a crisp bow and, for a finishing touch, add a sweet note of instructions.

To celebrate a wedding-to-be, give a couples' shower and ask everyone to bring a very special bottle of wine or champagne. This will result in the beginning of a wonderful wine cellar for the newlyweds.

For a very special wedding gift, have an artist paint the bride's bouquet so it will always look just picked. Wrap the painting in green florist tissue paper and tie it with a white satin ribbon. Tuck an artist's paintbrush and a flower through the bow.

For another twist on what to give the bride and groom: Rescue a few of their wedding flowers, press them, arrange them in a border around their wedding invitation, and frame it. Ask your local wallpaper store for its old wallpaper books and use the prettiest pages to wrap this special gift.

A perfect wedding gift for the bride and groom is to pack a delicious and romantic picnic supper. After the reception, when they are finally alone together, they'll have time to relax and enjoy your tasteful surprise.

A cookie jar filled with favorite recipe cards makes a dandy bridal shower or wedding gift.

For the bride and groom, create a unique photo album. Place a progression of pictures—showing each of them at different ages, baby to adult—paired on opposite pages of the album. Display it at the wedding reception.

Save squares of paper from all the gifts given at a bridal shower and fold each one into an origami (Japanese paper folding) design. Put them in a beautiful box and give them to the bride and groom for a wedding present.

For a keepsake first anniversary gift, make
a wreath decorated with tiny mementos of
the couple's wedding day—dried flowers
from the bride's bouquet, a flower from the
groom's boutonniere, a toy pocket-watch
set at the exact time that they said "I do,"
ribbons touting the wedding colors,
and so on.

Give the mothers of the bride and groom pampering gifts to be opened the day after the wedding.

To celebrate your first anniversary, put together a group of gifts that conjures up your honeymoon trip. For example, if you traveled to Venice, include a video of *An Afternoon in Venice*, a gift certificate for a two-hour canoe rental, a bottle of Italian wine, a vase made of Venetian glass, and a beautiful book on Venice.

Want to send your spouse a memorable anniversary gift? For the entire year following your next anniversary, have flowers, candy or lingerie delivered every month on your anniversary day—October 10th, November 10th, December 10th, etc. You'll be hearing fresh "thank you's" throughout the entire year ahead.

You have a *winning* marriage, why not give your spouse a beautiful trophy for an anniversary gift? Have an appropriate piece of sculpture or a lovely blown-glass vase mounted on a base. Engrave a small brass plate with the lovely sentiment:

To the man/woman who is always first in my heart.

Gifts

F O R

Special

Moments

After dinner at friends', slip into their kitchen and leave a thank you note— attached with a beautiful magnet on their fridge. It will make those stacks of dishes seem worthwhile.

If you know someone starting a new business or career, buy her a subscription to a trade magazine or newspaper in the area of her specialty.

If you know someone who has accomplished a personal goal or triumphed over adversity, give him a token gift that personifies what he has achieved—a gavel, for justice or personal power . . . a piece of hand blown glass for someone who has gone through fire and come out beautiful and strong. . . .

When you give a book as a gift, press a flower between the pages in the middle of the book. This makes an extra delightful surprise for the reader!

Always sign a gift book with a thoughtful note and date it—there's usually space on the first page. Pick out a passage in the book that reminds you of your friend, then mark it with a ribbon or a lovely bookmark.

On Halloween, take pictures of the neighborhood children who come knocking on your door. Next year display your "rogues gallery." And don't forget to take more pictures so you can continue the tradition.

For nostalgic gifts for babies, fill an album with pictures that illustrate what the world was like the year of their birth. For example, show the latest cars, clothes, food trends, perfumes, furniture, books, movies, musicians, computer games, sports stars, etc. Also include pictures of their parents, siblings, and pets. Newspaper headlines from major publications on the day they were born are always interesting and fun.

For someone opening a new office, a kaleidoscope is a great gift for her waiting room. For wrapping, use a mailing tube instead of a box. Place caps in both ends and cut a rectangle of wrapping paper several inches longer than the length of the tube. Wrap the paper completely around the tube and tie ribbons at each end to make it look like one of those old-fashioned birthday-party favors.

The perfect gift for a gift giver is a collection of beautiful wrapping papers, French ribbons and handmade gift cards. Enclose all of these lovelies in a plain, brown paper bag, turn the top down several times to make a collar, and tie it with brown kitchen twine. The contrast between the outside and the inside will be delightful.

And, lest we forget, the simplest and most thoughtful gift of all is a *Thank You* straight from the heart. That is what I send all of you for taking the time to read *Gifts from the Heart.* If you have a wonderfully thoughtful gift idea, I'd love to include it in my next book. Please send it along to:

Cynthia Whitney Ward
c/o Wings Books
40 Engelhard Avenue
Avenel, New Jersey 07001

Thank You!